Panic Disorder

Perspectives on Mental Health

by Nancy M. Campbell

Consultant:
Nina Holiday-Lynch, MA, LP
Psychologist
Fairview University Medical Center
Edina, Minnesota
Private Practice
Bloomington, Minnesota

LifeMatters
an imprint of Capstone Press
Mankato, Minnesota

LifeMatters Books are published by Capstone Press
PO Box 669 • 151 Good Counsel Drive • Mankato, Minnesota 56002
http://www.capstone-press.com

Printed in the United States of America

Library of Congress Cataloging-in-Publication Data
Campbell, Nancy M.
    Panic disorder / by Nancy M. Campbell.
        p.   cm. — (Perspectives on mental health)
    Includes bibliographical references and index.
    ISBN 0-7368-1030-7
    1. Panic attacks—Juvenile literature. 2. Anxiety—Juvenile literature. [1. Panic disorders. 2. Panic attacks. 3. Anxiety.] I. Title. II. Series.
    RC535 .C355 2002
    616.85'223—dc21   00-012937
                                                               CIP

Table of Contents

Chapter Overview

When people feel anxious, they're uneasy. They are worried that something they won't like might happen in the future.

A person feels fear when faced with a definite threat or danger. Fear triggers our fight-or-flight response. Fear turns to panic when the threat or danger overwhelms a person.

During a panic attack, intense fear suddenly overcomes a person. Yet no danger or threat is present.

Panic disorder is a treatable mental illness. One of its main symptoms is having repeated, full-blown panic attacks.

Chapter 1

Anxiety, Fear, and Panic

Anxiety

Anxiety is an uneasy feeling that something bad might occur. People who are anxious feel uncertain and on edge. They're not exactly sure what might happen, but they have a feeling that they won't like it. Anxiety is not focused on a well-defined danger. Instead, anxiety is a state of distress within a person about some vague or distant danger.

When asked how they're feeling, anxious people often say *uptight, tense, nervous,* or *worried*. Each of these words helps describe the feeling of anxiety. Anxious people often cannot specify what it is they're worried about.

We all feel anxiety at times. Anxiety is a natural human emotion like happiness, excitement, and anger. Anxiety ranges in intensity from mild to severe. In its mildest form, anxiety may be only a brief feeling of uncertainty. For example, some people feel mild anxiety when the power flickers off and on. Anxiety in its most severe form, however, can be a feeling of overwhelming terror. Most anxiety is not this extreme.

Our body often shows signs of our anxiety. If you're anxious while getting ready for a date, you may become jittery, or make fast, repetitive movements. You may become sweaty. Some other bodily signs of anxiety are tense muscles, faster breathing, and headaches. When anxiety lingers on for days or weeks, some people have trouble falling asleep at night.

The effects of anxiety can be positive or negative. For example, a gymnast may be anxious about falling from the balance beam. Her anxiety might heighten her senses to be more focused. This increased awareness and alertness could help her move with good form, timing, and balance. On the other hand, the gymnast's anxiety could disturb her concentration. She may be unsteady, tense up, or move with jerky hesitations that lead to a fall.

In whatever form or intensity it appears, anxiety is not pleasant. People who are anxious are uncomfortable and want the feeling to end.

Fear

Unlike anxiety, fear is a feeling people have when faced with an obvious danger that is threatening them. The danger is something clear-cut and something to which they can respond. For example, fear is felt when someone grabs you on a dark street or you wake up to the smell of smoke. In each case, you're aware of a real danger that threatens your well-being.

Fear triggers a person's natural fight-or-flight response. This is a response to real danger. First, the body experiences symptoms such as shakiness, a feeling of being out of control, and rapid breathing. Then, the brain reacts to the feeling of danger. It instantly causes the nervous system to release a surge of the hormone adrenaline. Hormones are chemicals that control various body processes. Adrenaline and related hormones rapidly move the body to a state of super-readiness. The body's heart and breathing rates, blood pressure, and muscle tension continue to increase. The body and brain are prepared to either face and fight the threatening danger or run from it.

The word *panic* comes from the name *Pan*. This Greek god of woods and fields supposedly caused the fear travelers felt in lonely areas.

Panic

It's possible for fear to grow into a state of extreme anxiety known as panic. Feeling panic is a totally different experience than feeling fear. Panic happens when the specific danger that is feared becomes overwhelming.

Consider this classic example. One wolf running down a hill to attack us would trigger fear. Our fight-or-flight response would send us racing in the opposite direction. But let's say six snarling wolves surround us and begin to close in. Suddenly, we have too many specific dangers to handle. We can no longer identify a route to safety. Our fear then erupts into panic.

The body's response can be dramatic when anxiety reaches the level of panic. Some experts think that the fight-or-flight response kicks into overdrive. We often overreact to the automatic increases in heart rate, blood pressure, and so on. Terrified, we may be unable to speak or move.

During panic, thinking and logic collapse, and disorganization sets in. Our behavior during panic often makes no sense. For example, we may wave our arms or legs about wildly, rush toward the danger, or laugh uncontrollably.

Panic Disorder

Panic Attacks

CHARLENE, AGE 15

Charlene and Roxie are sitting in the pretzel shop at the mall. Charlene's happy. She just bought a T-shirt and some shoes. Right now, Charlene is listening to Roxie complain about her younger brother. Suddenly, Charlene quits listening because she has started to sweat and is trembling. She feels a sense of danger spreading through her body. She notices that her heart is beating faster, which frightens her even more. Charlene glances about in all directions. Roxie is still talking and nothing seems wrong anywhere.

Trying to calm down, Charlene tells herself she's in no danger and to chill out. But now she feels like she's going to throw up. She's sure something bad is about to occur. She wonders, "What's happening to me?" But her fear continues and soon mounts to a terror she could never have imagined. Everything feels out of control, and nothing seems real.

All at once, Charlene has a strong urge to get far away. Sliding off her stool, she grabs her packages. Motioning Roxie to follow, Charlene walks rapidly toward the mall's nearest exit. Almost as soon as she's out of the mall, her terror eases up. By the time she sits down outside, her fear of danger has faded greatly. The frightening sensations in her body are calming down, too.

Feeling weak and puzzled, Charlene starts to explain what happened to wide-eyed Roxie. But she can't. Charlene has no idea what just happened herself.

People who have panic attacks often feel alone in their experience.

Charlene was having a panic attack, which is the most extreme form of anxiety. A panic attack is a sudden, overwhelming fear that comes without warning and for no clear reason. Panic attacks also are called anxiety attacks.

Normally, fear and panic are responses to clear-cut and present dangers or threats. However, the fear in a panic attack is different. It strikes without any clear and present danger. This is what makes the attacks so bewildering and embarrassing to the people who have them.

After several panic attacks, people usually are aware of the absence of danger during their attacks. But even so, they cannot stop their overwhelming fear during attacks that follow. Understandably, many people who have panic attacks begin to think something must be wrong with them. They may feel isolated and alone and usually are unable to talk about their attacks.

Panic Disorder

During a panic attack, a person's body and mind react as if the unknown danger were real. The symptoms of a panic attack include:

- Shortness of breath

- Rapid heartbeat or palpitations (pounding)

- Sense of choking or smothering

- Chest pain

- Unsteadiness, dizziness, or feeling of faintness

- Trembling or shaking

- Numbness or tingling

- Sweating

- Hot or cold flashes

- Nausea (feeling the need to throw up) or stomach pains

- Feeling of being disconnected from reality

- Fear of losing control or "going crazy"

- Fear of dying

In a full-blown panic attack, four or more of these bodily symptoms must be present at the same time. Most panic attacks last only two or three minutes and taper off fairly quickly. However, some attacks last up to 10 minutes. Rarely, attacks may last even up to an hour. Having only two or three of the symptoms is referred to as having a limited-symptom attack.

Panic disorder is a serious illness that affects at least
1 out of every 75 people worldwide. In the United
States, panic disorder affects more people each year
than does stroke, epilepsy, or AIDS.

Panic Disorder

Many people have one or two panic attacks in their life.
Researchers estimate that panic attacks strike one out of every
three people each year. But most people who have one or two
panic attacks do not have further attacks.

A person who has repeated panic attacks, however, may have a
treatable illness. This illness is called panic disorder. The
American Psychiatric Association (APA) has established the
following criteria, or standards, for defining panic disorder:

The person who has panic disorder must have had two or
more panic attacks.

These attacks must be full-blown and not limited-symptom
attacks.

At least one attack is followed by one month or more of
continuing worry about having another panic attack.

The attacks are not effects of a medical condition or a drug.

Panic attacks may last from 2 to 10 minutes. However, the uncomfortable symptoms may make them seem to last much longer.

Points to Consider

Think about people you know well and times when you thought they seemed anxious. What bodily signs gave you clues that they were anxious?

Think about times when you've been anxious. How does your body react when you're anxious?

The automatic fight-or-flight response often came to the aid of our ancient ancestors when wild animals threatened them. What kinds of situations are likely to set off our fight-or-flight response today?

Why might a person who has panic attacks be embarrassed by them?

Chapter Overview

Panic disorder often becomes more advanced. Complications can include anticipatory anxiety, avoidance behavior, and agoraphobia.

A majority of those people with panic disorder develop anticipatory anxiety. They fear future attacks.

Avoidance behavior means people with panic disorder avoid situations, places, or people believed to have triggered a panic attack.

Panic disorder with agoraphobia is the most serious and crippling complication. It causes a person to fear a wide variety of public places.

Chapter 2
Complications of Panic Disorder

Pure panic disorder is panic disorder without any complications. However, if nothing is done about the panic attacks a person with panic disorder has, serious complications may develop. Then, panic disorder becomes more advanced or complex.

Anticipatory Anxiety

After several panic attacks, most people begin to fear the terrifying feelings they have during their attacks. Often this is referred to as "fearing the fear." These people become apprehensive, or anxious, between panic attacks. They worry more and more about having another attack. Anxiety that is triggered by merely thinking about the possibility of having another attack is called "anticipatory anxiety." The anxious person is anticipating, or expecting, another attack to occur.

Research shows that 75 to 90 percent of those with panic disorder develop the life-changing complication of avoidance behavior.

Avoidance Behavior

Most people who have panic disorder want to prevent further attacks from happening. They soon try to figure out what triggers their attacks. Then they may begin to avoid some of the places or situations that might be setting off their attacks. For example, these people might stop going to a certain restaurant if an attack occurred inside or near it.

Some people with panic disorder feel on guard and tense most of their day. But their avoidance behavior doesn't stop the attacks from coming. In fact, the more vigilant, or watchful, these people become, the more likely they are to have panic attacks. As the attacks continue, the person's fear of them mounts. In turn, this growing fear increases the person's anticipatory anxiety and avoidance behavior.

Most avoidance behavior begins to change people's normal life. For example, they might discontinue going to a favorite hangout. They might even quit being around friends who were present during one of their attacks. Some people also avoid things that bring on any of the physical symptoms they have during attacks. For example, some people give up jogging because it brings on shortness of breath. People's home, school, work, and social life all can be severely limited.

Something as simple as rain may make it hard for a person with avoidance behavior to leave his or her home.

Elaine's first panic attack happened one day after school.

ELAINE, AGE 16

She had been walking home in the rain. Her next attack came while she was watching TV. Soon she couldn't stop worrying about where and when her next attack would occur. When she had another attack while watching TV, she stopped watching TV altogether.

But the attacks continued. Elaine tried to remember all the details of her former attacks. She felt on guard and tense most of the time. Gradually, she stopped walking home after school. Eventually, she decided she couldn't risk going out in the rain. A few times, she even refused to go out when the skies were cloudy.

Sometimes a person's fear of attacks and avoidance behavior become so extreme they lead to a phobia. A phobia is a continuing unreasonable and exaggerated fear. People with panic disorder can become phobic about any of the objects or situations they're avoiding. Phobic avoidance behavior can be harder on people than avoidance behavior alone.

About 30 to 40 percent of all people with panic disorder develop an early stage of agoraphobia.

Agoraphobia

The most serious complication of panic disorder is known as panic disorder with agoraphobia, or PDA. *Agoraphobia* means "fear of public places."

People with PDA have an extreme fear of having a panic attack in a public place. They avoid a wide variety of specific situations. For example, most people with PDA fear being trapped or unable to get help during a panic attack. They fear having an attack in a place or situation from which getting away might be difficult. These people usually fear embarrassment as well. They don't want others to see them having a panic attack. People with PDA are especially sensitive to either small or wide-open places.

Many people with PDA avoid places and situations that are crowded or that might become crowded. Some common places they avoid are busy restaurants, grocery stores, and shopping malls. Others are large athletic, cultural, and social events.

Other people with PDA may refuse to be in certain types of enclosed spaces. Commonly, these places include elevators, tunnels, and public transportation such as buses, trains, subways, and planes. All of these are spaces in which a person could become trapped and unable to get away during a panic attack.

Early detection significantly reduces the complications of untreated panic disorder. Appropriate psychiatric, or mental health, treatment can help. Up to 90 percent of people with panic disorder recover and return to normal life activities after psychiatric treatment.

Many people with PDA simply have great anxiety about being far from home in general. Some have strict limits, such as a five-mile or five-kilometer radius, beyond which they will not go.

Less often, people with PDA are afraid of being alone. They don't feel safe unless they're with certain people. They may become dependent on a particular person. They may need this person to do everyday errands with them, such as going to the grocery store. Without a clear understanding of PDA, this situation can become frustrating and exhausting for those involved.

In the rarest and most severe cases, people with PDA become completely housebound. Their fear of a panic attack becomes extreme. These people may lock their doors, cover their windows, and avoid seeing the outside world. This crippling state often leads to serious depression and a high risk of suicide, or killing oneself.

Points to Consider

Most people with panic disorder begin avoiding places and situations they think might be triggering their attacks. Why might this be difficult for them?

If one of your friends started avoiding you, how would you feel? What would you think of that friend?

If you had a friend who had panic disorder with agoraphobia, how might you help him or her?

Panic disorder can affect anyone. The most common time for panic disorder to begin is between the late teen years and the early twenties.

Both biological and psychological causes have been linked to panic disorder. Most researchers think many of the disease's possible causes overlap and interact with each other.

Panic attacks aren't dangerous. They cannot cause a person to choke, "go crazy," or die. However, substance abuse and depression can develop with panic disorder and may cause harm.

A person who thinks he or she may have panic disorder should see a doctor. It's important that other possible medical reasons for panic attacks be ruled out. Then, the person can see a mental health professional.

Chapter **3**

Common Questions About Panic Disorder

You may have questions about panic disorder. You also may have questions about panic attacks, which are the key symptom of the disorder. This chapter answers some of the common questions most people have.

Who Gets Panic Disorder?

Panic disorder can occur in just about anyone. The illness affects people of all ethnic groups, family backgrounds, and social and economic status. Panic disorder now is being studied in many countries around the world. Researchers report that the illness is equally common in every country.

Many studies indicate that the tendency to have panic disorder can be inherited. If your parent or a brother or sister has panic disorder, your own chance of developing it increases by four to eight times.

Panic disorder usually begins between the late teen years and early twenties. It begins only rarely during childhood or after age 45. Females get panic disorder about two times more often than males do. Females have the more advanced condition of panic disorder with agoraphobia three times more often than males do. The reason for this gender difference is still under investigation.

What Causes Panic Disorder?
A variety of causes have been linked to panic disorder. Today, most experts believe that both biological and psychological factors play a role in causing the illness. Biological causes are physical. Psychological causes are things that affect the mind and behavior.

Panic disorder is a complex illness because the actual combination of causes varies from person to person. Also, most researchers think many of the disorder's possible causes overlap and interact with each other. Scientists are studying how these causes work with each other. This will help scientists learn more about how the body and mind work together in this disease.

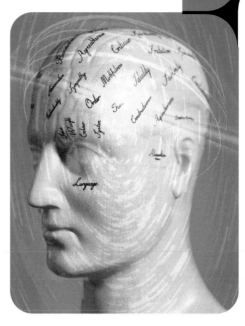

An imbalance of brain chemicals may be one possible cause of panic disorder.

Biological Causes

The biological causes of panic disorder are based in a person's heredity and brain chemistry. Heredity is the passing down of traits, or characteristics, from parents to their children.

Heredity. Traits are carried from parent to child by genes in the blood. A tendency to develop panic disorder may be inherited in this way. For this reason, panic disorder is said to run in families. However, not everyone with a family history of panic disorder develops the illness. Many people without a family history of panic disorder also develop the illness.

Brain chemistry. Some scientists investigate the biological causes of diseases. These scientists look for physical and chemical imbalances in the brain and body. Many of their studies show that chemical imbalances in the brain may be a possible cause of panic disorder. Some of the evidence is based on certain medications that relieve some people's symptoms of the disorder. The medications that best do this are antidepressants that change the levels of certain brain chemicals.

Psychological Causes

Most of the psychological causes of panic disorder are connected to the stress in a person's life.

Childhood experiences. Studies show that many people with panic disorder recall stressful, unhappy, or even traumatic, or shocking, childhood experiences. One such experience is the early loss of a parent through death or separation. Other experiences are having a long childhood illness or an extreme fright, such as a fire in the home. A child may experience growing up with an alcoholic, drug dependent, or negative and critical parent. This can lead to severe anxieties. Living with a physically or sexually abusive parent is devastating for a child.

All of these experiences increase the chance that panic disorder will surface when the child is older. This is true especially if the child has inherited the tendency toward panic disorder.

Major life changes. Major events in life can be powerful triggers of anxiety. Some examples are turning points such as graduation, divorce, marriage, a birth, a promotion, or loss of employment. Others can be a geographic move, a serious illness, a financial loss or gain, a disability, or sudden fame.

A life-changing event may be positive or negative. The anxiety usually comes from adjustments or transitions that are made because of the change. Many people with panic disorder report going through a major life change in the month before their first panic attack.

Major changes in life, such as graduation, may cause stress and trigger anxiety, leading to panic disorder.

Martina usually is laid back, but lately she's been feeling

MARTINA, AGE 18

impatient and irritable. She has been getting headaches and is having trouble sleeping. She's puzzled. It's not at all like her. She tries to ignore it. But as the weeks go by, Martina becomes more and more touchy and out of sorts.

Martina is experiencing a growing anxiety because of some upcoming changes in her life. Right after graduation she'll be working full-time at the lumberyard. She's not sure she'll like the job. Also, her best friend, Amanda, is moving out of state at the end of July. Martina senses that other changes and new responsibilities could be cropping up. But she has no idea what they might be.

Extended periods of stress. The influence of repeated or extended periods of stress also plays a role in the development of panic disorder. Stress tends to build up when it stretches out without relief for many years. Relationships, school, sports, jobs, abuse, and divorce all are things that can cause stress. Long-term stress sometimes comes from the same source. For example, a person may experience continuing problems at home or school. Stress from a variety of sources also may build up over time. Periods of stress that extend over one or two years can be draining and may lead to exhaustion.

Even without addiction, large amounts of marijuana or cocaine are toxic and can trigger panic. In addicted teens, withdrawal from alcohol or certain drugs called narcotics also can trigger panic.

Are Panic Attacks Dangerous?

Panic attacks in themselves are not dangerous. Although a panic attack is terrifying, it will not harm you physically or increase your risk of death. You or someone you know may be highly distressed and frightened by the intense physical symptoms of panic attacks. But remember to keep in mind the following facts about panic attacks:

They themselves are not dangerous.

They cannot cause a heart attack.

They won't cause you to stop breathing.

They will not cause you to lose your balance or fall.

They cannot cause you to "lose control of yourself."

They cannot cause you to "go crazy."

Individual panic attacks are not dangerous. Panic disorder, however, often is coupled with substance abuse or depression. In these cases, some potentially dangerous and even fatal situations can develop.

People with panic disorder may turn to alcohol or other drugs for relief. However, in the long run, this may lead to increased anxiety or chemical dependence.

Alcohol and Drug Abuse

The danger of alcohol and drug abuse is a two-way street. A person's use of alcohol or other drugs can trigger his or her first panic attack. On the other hand, some people with panic disorder try alcohol or drugs to calm their fears and anxieties. For a time, these chemicals do bring relief. This happens because one of the first effects of alcohol and some drugs is to lessen tension. This quick relief easily can lead people with panic disorder to use the alcohol or drugs more frequently. But heavier use may increase the frequency of panic attacks. Soon, a repeating pattern of more attacks, higher anxiety, and heavier use is in place.

Substance abuse and addiction are sneaky. There are no warning bells or red flags. Some people with panic disorder seeking relief eventually slip into chemical dependency. When this occurs, the person has two serious problems needing treatment.

Depression

Some people struggle with depression before they begin having panic attacks. Other people become depressed after experiencing regular panic attacks. Either way, when depression exists with panic disorder, treatment for panic disorder is complicated and slowed, if not impossible.

Some people see several medical doctors about their frightening symptoms. These people even may have rushed to the emergency room because of their symptoms. And each time, they may be told that nothing is physically wrong. This isn't unusual. Many people with panic disorder go through this same thing. This frustrating experience sometimes occurs because not all doctors are trained to notice or look for mental disorders.

The most important issue about depression and panic disorder is the higher chance of suicide. If anyone has or may have panic disorder, this fatal possibility must not be ignored. Seeking proper diagnosis, or determination of the disorder, and treatment can be lifesaving.

How Can I Find Out If I Have Panic Disorder?

Repeated panic attacks are the key symptom of panic disorder. If you think you have suffered several panic attacks, take action to find out for sure.

Diagnosing panic disorder can be difficult. Many of its symptoms are the same as those of other medical conditions and diseases. Some of these are hypoglycemia (low blood sugar), hyperthyroidism (overactive thyroid gland), and certain brain and heart diseases. These other medical problems must be ruled out before a diagnosis of panic disorder can be made.

The first step is to make an appointment with a doctor for a full medical examination. It's important to make sure that this doctor is familiar with panic disorder. At the appointment, describe your symptoms and explain that you're trying to find out if you have panic disorder. Tell your doctor you would like to be checked for any other medical condition that might be causing your symptoms. If the other conditions are ruled out, then seek further diagnosis from a qualified mental health professional. Your doctor may be able to help you locate this person.

Psychiatrists and psychologists are the most qualified professionals to diagnose panic disorder. Psychiatrists are medical doctors. They specialize in diseases and disorders of the mind. They're well trained to separate the physical and mental aspects of a person's symptoms. Psychologists are trained to test and diagnose for mental illnesses. Licensed clinical social workers are qualified to diagnose panic disorder as well.

Points to Consider

Two children of a parent with panic disorder may likely inherit a tendency to develop the illness. Why might one child get the disease while the other one doesn't?

How could getting married lead to a person's first panic attack?

Some people with panic disorder also are chemically dependent or depressed. Why do you think it's often necessary to treat the chemical dependency or depression before treating the panic disorder?

Teens differ in how they react to their first panic attack.

Panic disorder can affect a teen's relationships seriously. Friends can be confused, hurt, and angered. Sometimes relationships even fall apart.

Teens with panic disorder may limit their activities to try to avoid panic attacks. Their performance at school, sports, or jobs may suffer because of their anxiety.

Confusion is the most common reaction of others to a teen who has had a panic attack. Otherwise, the reactions are widely mixed and changing. Many people want to offer help and support.

Chapter 4

Panic Disorder in a Teen's Life

Teens differ in how they respond to their first panic attack. Many rush straight to an emergency room. They may be convinced their life or sanity is about to end. These teens may be perplexed and then worried when nothing is found to be life threatening. Other teens may be frightened after their first panic attack. However, they may think the attack was something odd that wouldn't happen again.

Most teens are shaken and confused by their first panic attack. If they have several attacks, they soon realize that no real danger is present during their attacks. Even so, they cannot stop the terror that continues to overwhelm them. They cannot explain these terrified feelings and may be deeply embarrassed by them.

Teens may feel isolated if their panic disorder begins to affect their relationships.

Because of their confusion and embarrassment, most teens try to hide their disorder from others. They don't want anyone to know about their attacks—not even their family members or best friends.

How Panic Disorder Can Affect a Teen's Life

Panic disorder changes a teen's life in many ways. The illness can seriously affect a teen's relationships, activities and performance, and sense of self.

Relationships

When teens keep their panic attacks a secret, they bottle up their thoughts and feelings. Doing this causes most teens to feel distant from other people. Soon their relationships may not feel quite right. The teen may feel cut off from others.

Panic disorder often is complicated by avoidance behavior at some point. Many teens with panic disorder begin avoiding certain events or situations they think may bring on a panic attack. These teens may try to disguise or make excuses for their avoidance behavior. But almost always, their excuses seem strange to others. Friends may feel hurt or offended. Angry arguments sometimes flare up. If the truth doesn't come out, friendships can be strained seriously or even broken.

Some teens with panic disorder fear that being near a certain person might trigger a panic attack. While they may not want to, they usually begin to avoid this person. Many relationships fall apart quickly if this happens. Avoiding close friends and family members is difficult if not impossible. Sometimes avoiding a person cannot be done. This can be almost unbearable for teens because of their fear that a panic attack may happen at any time. Teens in this situation often are highly upset and distressed or irritable.

Activities and Performance

Most teens with panic disorder begin limiting where they go and what they do. Normal daily activities may change, or certain activities may be dropped altogether. For example, a teen may spend more time at home instead of going to movies or riding around with friends. Other regular activities such as shopping or going to ball games may become off limits, too.

Anxiety about attacks also can affect a teen's concentration and performance. Playing the piano, solving puzzles, taking tests, even remembering tasks may become harder to do. The teen's performance in school, in sports, and at a job may suffer.

"It's such a relief to know that what I have is an illness.
And it has a name that makes sense—*panic disorder*.
Honestly, I had been feeling like I was a total freak!"
—Stacy, age 16

Sense of Self

Having panic disorder usually changes a teen's view of himself or
herself. Most teens lose self-confidence and self-esteem when
they're unable to stop their panic attacks. Many see themselves as
cowardly or lacking in willpower, or energetic determination.

Because there seems to be no reason for the illness, many teens
worry that it's their own fault. They may view themselves as bad
people. However, none of this is true. People do not bring on their
own panic disorder. No person has panic disorder because of a
lack of courage or a fault or failing of character. People with
panic disorder simply have an illness. This illness can be treated,
and recovery is possible.

How Others May React

People with panic disorder often worry about others' reactions to
hearing about or seeing one of their panic attacks. Many teens
assume reactions will be negative and painful to them. This can
happen. But many reactions aren't negative or hurtful. The most
common reaction of others is confusion. Otherwise, there's a wide
range of reactions.

Reactions are different, depending on what people know about the
illness. It helps for people with panic disorder to be prepared for
mixed and changing reactions to their illness. Some people who
aren't familiar with panic disorder may think a person having a
panic attack is weird. Some may think it's strange that a person
can be so afraid when there's no danger. On the other hand, some
people know about the illness. They may think a person is
unlucky to have this condition. They may understand what the
person is going through and offer help and support.

Most people want to offer support when they find out a friend or family member has panic disorder.

CAITLIN, AGE 14

Caitlin's panic attacks really embarrass her. At first, she tried to ignore them, thinking they would just go away. But a new attack hit her about every six weeks. Caitlin tried to predict what triggered her attacks, but she always was way off. Caitlin started to lose confidence in herself. She came to believe she was slowly losing her mind.

A few months ago, Caitlin's best friend was able to help her start talking about her problem. Caitlin couldn't look into her friend's eyes. But with her friend's encouragement, she began looking for treatment.

Points to Consider

How do you think teens feel when they are successful in keeping their panic attacks a secret from others? Why do you think they may feel this way?

What do you think is the worst way a teen with panic disorder is affected by the illness? Explain.

Have you ever heard about or seen someone having a panic attack? If so, how did you react? If not, how do you think you would react?

Most often, a combination of cognitive behavioral therapy (CBT) and medication is used to treat panic disorder.

Cognitive behavioral therapy is a two-part approach to the treatment of panic disorder. The first part helps people discover and correct faulty beliefs that are causing anxiety. The second part involves teaching behaviors such as deep relaxation that can reduce anxiety.

The five key elements in CBT are: learning, monitoring, relaxing, rethinking, and exposing.

Some medications have proven to be helpful in treating panic disorder. Panic attacks can be reduced or even blocked by certain antidepressants and minor tranquilizers.

Chapter **5**

Treatment and Recovery

Panic disorder is a serious illness. It can disrupt a person's life. Fortunately, treatment for the disorder can be quite successful. With appropriate treatment, 75 to 90 percent of people with panic disorder recover. They are able to return to normal life activities.

People with panic disorder usually meet with a therapist for diagnosis and treatment. The therapist might be a psychiatrist, psychologist, mental health counselor, or clinical social worker. At the first appointment, the therapist asks questions about the person's background, family, personal habits, and general health. Symptoms are discussed in detail. They're checked carefully against the criteria for panic disorder developed by the APA. (The criteria are listed in Chapter 1.) Treatment options are explained to the person, and a treatment plan is made.

As a person is overcoming panic disorder, support from others is sometimes a vital part of the recovery process. With the person's permission, family and friends often are informed of the treatment plan. The therapist shares ways they can be most helpful.

During recovery, some people reach a point where they no longer anticipate the occurrence of panic attacks. When people no longer care whether they panic, the attacks eventually subside.

Two main treatment options have been successful with panic disorder. One is cognitive behavioral therapy, or CBT. The other treatment option is medication. Often, a combination of the two is used. The actual treatment for each individual depends on his or her preferences, medical history, and symptoms.

Cognitive Behavioral Therapy (CBT)

Cognitive behavioral therapy is a treatment approach that blends two other separate therapies. These are cognitive therapy and behavioral therapy.

Cognitive means "based on knowledge or what is known." The cognitive aspect of CBT looks at our beliefs and thoughts about the world, the future, and ourselves. This part of CBT helps people with panic disorder discover and correct the faulty or mistaken thoughts that are causing anxiety. The goal of the cognitive part of CBT is to change thinking to calm the mind.

The behavioral aspect of CBT helps people learn behaviors that can reduce anxiety. A daily program of relaxation, including deep breathing and exercise, is learned. The behavioral part of CBT works to change behavior to relax and calm the body.

People undergoing CBT usually begin to show improvement within six weeks or less. Therapy usually lasts about 12 weeks. Five key elements in CBT are: learning, monitoring, relaxing, rethinking, and exposing.

Learning
In the first stage, the therapist explains the illness. The therapist teaches the person with panic disorder to identify his or her own symptoms.

Monitoring
The person keeps a diary or log to keep track of his or her panic attacks. Situations that trigger anxiety are recorded.

Relaxing
The therapist teaches the person relaxation techniques. One method may be breathing slowly and deeply from the abdomen. Relaxation combats the physical symptoms of a panic attack.

Rethinking

The therapist helps the person see how faulty thinking patterns contribute to anxiety. The person learns to identify and change his or her faulty thinking patterns. Two anxiety-producing thinking patterns are common for many people with panic disorder. These are anxious or negative self-talk and illogical or mistaken thoughts and beliefs.

Self-talk is what we say to ourselves in our own minds. Anxious or negative self-talk statements often create anxiety. This kind of self-talk even can set off a panic attack or make one worse. The therapist helps the person identify his or her negative self-talk and replace it with positive self-talk.

YOSA, AGE 15

Yosa has been in CBT for three weeks. Right now, he's working on catching his anxious self-talk. Once he can do that, he can replace those negative lines of thinking with more positive statements.

Yosa knows that his worst habit is using "What if" questions, such as "What if I lose control?" and "What if I can't survive this?" He's starting to see that he tends to anticipate the worst. This sometimes is called catastrophic thinking. Yosa also overestimates the odds of something bad happening. At these times, he asks himself, "Have I ever lost control?" His answer is no, which makes him feel less helpless.

Most anxious or negative self-talk can be traced back to deeper-lying illogical or mistaken thoughts and beliefs. These thoughts and beliefs are basic false assumptions about the self and life in general. Such beliefs often set limits on a person's confidence and self-esteem. The therapist can help the person replace each mistaken belief with a more accurate one.

STEPHANIE, AGE 13

Stephanie learned in CBT that she had several mistaken beliefs. Three of them were "I'm powerless," "If I take risks, I'll fail," and "The world is a dangerous place." Just recognizing these beliefs helped her begin to let go of them. She learned to develop affirmations, or positive statements, to counter her mistaken beliefs. For the first, she came up with, "I'm responsible and in control of my life." For the second, she used, "It's okay for me to take risks." She also used, "It's okay to fail—I can learn a lot from every mistake." For the third, she said, "I can learn to become more comfortable with the outside world."

Exposing

The therapist helps the person with panic disorder encounter situations that bring on frightening physical sensations. The encounters gradually increase in intensity at a pace that's comfortable for the person.

Many CBT therapists recommend a support group for some people with panic disorder. A support group with others who suffer from the same illness can be helpful to some people. Often, members of a support group gain new understanding about the illness and how to cope with it.

When seeking treatment for panic disorder, it's important to find a mental health professional with the right qualifications. Here are some questions you or your parents might want to ask before beginning treatment:

- How many people with panic disorder have you treated?

- Do you have special training for treating panic disorder?

- What approach do you use for treatment? (CBT, medication, both?)

- How long does treatment typically last?

- What do you charge?

- Can you help me determine if my health insurance will cover treatment?

Medication

Medication is an important treatment option for some people with panic disorder. Certain medications are known to help treat panic disorder. The most successful are specific antidepressants and antianxiety medications. Some antidepressants and minor tranquilizers that calm people can reduce or even block panic attacks. These medicines also can decrease anticipatory anxiety.

Medication can be used as the only treatment for panic disorder. It's most effective, however, when used as part of a treatment plan that involves therapy, as well.

The decision whether to use medication in the process of recovery is a big one. It's one that people and their doctor should make together. Several factors need to be considered. They include the severity of the illness, whether depression is present, physical health, and goals and preferences about treatment. Some people prefer not to take medication. Others are willing to try it.

People with panic disorder may see a medical doctor who monitors their medications.

Antidepressants generally take four to eight weeks before they are working fully. Usually, antidepressants are not physically addictive and side effects are minimal. Some antianxiety medications can be addictive. It's important that a psychiatrist or medical doctor closely monitors doses.

Points to Consider

In the first stage of CBT, the therapist explains panic disorder to the person who has it. In what ways might learning about the illness be helpful?

A person with panic disorder might be extremely distrustful. If so, what do you think might be some of his or her mistaken beliefs?

Why do you think therapists don't always suggest a support group for people with panic disorder?

Would you use medication as a treatment option for panic disorder? Why or why not?

Chapter
Overview

Chapter Overview

People with panic disorder can make significant contributions to trying to prevent panic.

Deep relaxation is a state that slows down many body processes. It lowers anxiety and reduces stress. Three ways to achieve deep relaxation are deep breathing from the abdomen, progressive muscle relaxation, and meditation. It's also important to take time out for yourself.

Lifestyle changes are an important way to relieve tension and reduce anxiety by improving physical health.

Chapter **6**

Working Toward Prevention

What needs to be done to help prevent panic is surprisingly simple. Underneath panic is anxiety. When you reduce anxiety, you can reduce panic. There are two excellent ways to reduce anxiety. One is to practice deep relaxation. The other is to improve your physical health by making a few lifestyle changes. A strong commitment to prevention is important. Prevention works most powerfully when it's done faithfully, every day.

Make Deep Relaxation a Daily Habit

Deep relaxation lowers anxiety and lessens the effects of stress. It promotes a sense of well-being. Practicing deep relaxation is more than lying around watching TV.

Learning to relax is important when trying to reduce anxiety.

Deep relaxation is a state that changes many body processes. It lowers heart and breathing rates and blood pressure. It decreases muscle tension, metabolism, and thought activity. Metabolism is the process by which the body changes food to energy. The state of deep relaxation is the exact opposite of the body's state during a panic attack.

To reach deep relaxation, practice one of the following methods for 20 to 30 minutes. If done daily for several weeks, you will tend to feel more relaxed all the time. Daily practice of deep relaxation can lessen your anxiety. In turn, this can lessen the frequency and severity of panic attacks.

Following are three ways to reach deep relaxation. It's fine to use the same method each day or to use a different one. Books that describe in detail how each method is done are available in stores and libraries.

Deep Breathing

When anxious, you tend to breathe with fairly fast, short breaths that come from high up in your chest. In deep breathing, breaths are full, slow, and gentle. They come from your lower chest and abdomen.

Here's how to practice deep breathing. Slowly and gently, breathe in through the nose for six slow counts. Pause for two counts. Then breathe out through the mouth for another six slow counts. While inhaling, or breathing in, imagine a sense of needed health and well-being coming into your body. While exhaling, or breathing out, imagine letting go of your sense of being on guard. Let the feeling of tension flow out of your body.

Progressive Muscle Relaxation

This well-known technique is sometimes called full-body relaxation. It relaxes the body by relieving muscle tension. In this technique, six different muscle groups are tensed and gradually relaxed individually for about 10 to 15 seconds. Usually, the hands and arms are done first. Then, starting from the feet and working up, the rest of the body is tensed and relaxed. These groupings are the feet and legs; the buttocks, abdomen, and lower back; the shoulders; the neck and throat; and the face and head. The buttocks are the fleshy part of the body where one sits.

Here are some means of relaxation that can be useful in coping with anxiety and stress:

- Yoga (a system of exercises for achieving well-being)

- Tai chi (an ancient physical art form that includes stretching, breathing, and circular motions)

- Visualization of peaceful scenes

- Making affirmations (positive statements about life and yourself)

- Massage

- Listening to special relaxation tapes

Meditation

Meditation is a specific way to rest the mind completely. All thinking, both about the past and future, is stopped. The mind is quiet and simply rests on each present moment. All sense of the outside world and the surrounding environment ceases. The breath becomes slow and deep. In meditation, the mind is clear, relaxed, and focused within yourself rather than on the outside world. Meditation usually is done in a seated position with the eyes closed.

Take Time for Yourself

Even taking just a few minutes each day for yourself can help you relax. What are some ways to relieve the stress of a busy day? Try playing piano, listening to music, drawing, writing in a journal, or being out in nature.

TERRELL, AGE 16

Terrell wanted to reduce his extreme anxiety. On and off, he had been attempting deep breathing, progressive muscle relaxation, and meditation. But nothing seemed to click. His anxiety even seemed worse. Then he decided to take things more seriously.

First, he committed himself to having a 20-minute relaxation session every day for three weeks. Second, he made one corner of his bedroom the place he would do all of his relaxation sessions. Third, he got some books out of the library that explained each of the methods in detail. Fourth, he read about and practiced only one method each week. Finally, he did all of his sessions at the same time each day. He chose the early morning when the house was still quiet. During the second week he started to feel calmer and looked forward to his session. During the third week, he felt noticeably more relaxed during much of his day.

Exercise can reduce tension and anxiety. It even can help relieve depression.

Make Needed Lifestyle Changes

Improving physical health can improve your mental health. This generally means less anxiety.

Get regular exercise. Regular exercise is a sure way to relieve tension and reduce anxiety. This is 20 to 30 minutes of exercise, three to five times per week. Running, walking, jogging, aerobics classes, bicycling, weight training, and swimming all are good choices. Regular exercise also can help relieve depression.

Don't smoke. Nicotine is a drug used in tobacco products such as cigarettes. It's a strong stimulant that increases heart rate, metabolism, and blood pressure. It also constricts, or squeezes, blood vessels around the heart. Nicotine can bring on a nervous or jittery feeling. Many smokers believe that having a cigarette calms their nerves. Research has proven, however, that smokers tend to be more anxious than nonsmokers are. Smokers usually don't sleep as well either.

Avoid other stimulants. Stimulants—especially caffeine, chocolate, and sugar—rev up the nervous system and increase anxiety. Stimulants can set the stage for a panic attack. Also beware of other stimulants. These include diet pills, stay-awake aids, decongestants that help relieve stuffiness, and cold remedies.

"Being with others helps me relax. I've decided to add two social activities to my personal plan for preventing anxiety. One is to join a support group for people with panic disorder. The other is to spend time each week with at least two other people who are important to me."—Gina, age 15

Eat healthy foods. Fresh, whole foods can have a calming effect on the body. Eat plenty of fruits, vegetables, proteins, and whole grains. Drink more water. Avoid processed, boxed foods with additives and preservatives. These are chemicals added to foods to add flavor and color and to maintain freshness.

Get enough sleep. Starting each day rested and refreshed helps you handle the tensions and fears that can bring on panic. It's important that you get as much rest as you need. Most teens need 8 to 10 hours of sleep each night.

Avoid alcohol and other drugs. Avoid the risk and danger of substance abuse, which often can grow out of panic disorder. Even without abuse, using alcohol and other drugs increases anxiety in the long run.

Points to Consider

How do you think practicing deep relaxation regularly can lower anxiety and lessen the effects of stress? What impact might it have on the body?

What could you do to lessen anxiety?

Many people have a hard time sticking to their plans for making needed lifestyle changes. What might be some reasons for this? What could people do to overcome these difficulties?

Many people with panic disorder find it useful to keep handy a short list on a note card. Listed are the most effective things to focus on when trying to cope with panic disorder.

If early symptoms of panic begin, it's easy to get rattled. An ABC prompt can help remind you what to do: Accept symptoms/Avoid fighting them → Breathe → Cope.

Sometimes it's hard to avoid a panic attack, even though you may try to catch the early symptoms. In this case, move away from the current situation if possible. Then, the ABC prompt can be tried again.

The acceptance and support of family and friends can be important to a person with panic disorder.

Chapter **7**

Steps to Take—For You, Family, and Friends

What You Can Do Right Now

Many people with panic disorder often say, "What can I do right now?" You may want to write down the list of suggestions on the next page on two small cards. Keep one in a safe place and carry the other one with you. Glancing at the card can help you remember what you can do to avoid panic. The card serves as a reminder that the best things to do are not fancy. The suggestions on the next page are very basic.

Breathe deeply and slowly.

Find out as many facts as possible about panic disorder.

Exercise regularly.

Avoid nicotine and other stimulants.

Eat fresh, whole foods.

Stay away from alcohol and other drugs.

Identify your early symptoms—those that occur before attacks—and be ready to take action if needed.

What to Do If Early Symptoms Begin

Take the following steps as soon as possible if any of your early symptoms arise. Remember to follow this general ABC order: Accept symptoms/Avoid fighting them → Breathe → Cope.

Accept and Avoid

First, accept that your symptoms are happening. But move on and avoid letting yourself get caught up in them. Avoid trying to fight your symptoms or stop them. Fighting anxiety symptoms tends to make them worse.

Breathe

Second, start taking slow, deep breaths. Concentrate on the slowness and deepness of your breathing. Count to six as you inhale through your nose. Pause. Count to six as you exhale through your mouth. Do this for at least three minutes.

Cope

Third, try any of the following coping strategies.

Move around and get active. Exercise. Dance. Go outside.

Sing a song, either aloud or to yourself.

Focus on the details of objects around you. Study colors, textures, lines, curves, and so on. Touch the objects or the floor or ground. This can help keep you in the present.

Take a bath or shower. Wash your hair or your face. Brush your teeth.

Do something with your hands. Cook. Water your plants or garden. Play solitaire. Beat out a drumming pattern.

Repeat your favorite coping statements. You may want to write them on a card and keep it with you if they're hard to remember. Here are some examples of coping statements. "This isn't dangerous." "This will pass in a few minutes, and I'll be okay." "I can accept this situation and ride it out." Or, you can use positive statements as if you were a person who doesn't have panic attacks. For example, "I have many coping strengths such as. . . . And I am living a happy life without panic."

Tell yourself some jokes or riddles. Read something aloud.

Start talking with someone (by phone if necessary).

Do anything else that helps distract you from your symptoms.

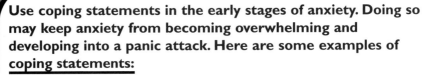

AT A GLANCE

Use coping statements in the early stages of anxiety. Doing so may keep anxiety from becoming overwhelming and developing into a panic attack. Here are some examples of coping statements:

- I can do it.

- I can handle it.

- I can cope.

- Easy does it.

- My heartbeat speeds up when I'm stressed, and that's okay.

- I'm a little tense today, but it will pass.

- Anxiety doesn't kill anyone.

- I can distract myself.

- I'm relaxing my muscles.

- Each time I face my fear, I feel stronger.

What to Do During a Panic Attack

Sometimes, you may not be able to avoid a panic attack by stopping your early symptoms. If a panic attack develops, move away from whatever situation you are in if possible. Then, repeat the ABC steps.

Tips for Family and Friends Who Want to Help

You can make a difference in the life of someone with panic disorder. Your acceptance and support can be important to the person. Realizing that recovery is a process may help you to be understanding. This recovery process may be short or long.

Remember that all the fears, feelings, and "what ifs" are very real to the person with panic disorder. It is not useful to say, "It's all in your head." People with panic disorder know these feelings are going on inside them. They can be extremely embarrassed by this. They may feel frustration, guilt, shame, or depression.

Your support
can make
a difference
in the life of
someone
who has
panic
disorder.

As a person who can provide support, keep the following tips
in mind:

Educate yourself about panic attacks, panic disorder, and
their treatment. Learn about the symptoms, fears, and
feelings that go on within a person who has this illness.

Be available, positive, and patient.

Listen when the person needs to talk.

Let the person tell you what she or he can do and how she
or he would like you to act.

Encourage the person's attempts at self-help and
independence.

Notice and compliment the person's efforts.

The role of a support person can be tiring, frustrating, confusing, and very time-consuming. Being properly prepared about the illness can help.

Allow the person to be in charge of his or her own recovery.

Honor the person's wishes about confidentiality, or privacy.

Avoid expressing disappointment, anger, or frustration.

Avoid letting the person down by making promises you can't keep.

Avoid surprises. Let the person know what's going to happen and when. This allows him or her to make plans to deal with panic that may arise.

Don't feel guilty if the person has a panic attack or doesn't seem to be getting better. This isn't your fault.

Take time for yourself. Don't let your entire life revolve around the person's illness.

Have someone such as a close friend, trusted adult, or counselor whom you can go to for support and advice.

Look for support groups for yourself. One source for finding such groups is at *www.pacificcoast.net/~kstrong*.

LaTonya was just diagnosed with

panic disorder. Her best friend, Marshall, wanted to do anything he could to help her. So he asked her about the illness and also read some information about it on the Internet.

One day, he and LaTonya were standing outside an ice cream shop when she had an attack. LaTonya quickly crouched down to the sidewalk, knocking a metal chair down with her. She let out a wailing sound as terror flooded over her. Two kids from school were there and started making fun of LaTonya. Marshall spoke up and told the two girls that LaTonya had an illness. "Would you make fun of somebody with cancer?" he asked. The two girls seemed embarrassed. They said "Sorry" quietly and walked away.

Marshall turned his attention back to LaTonya, who was already coming out of her attack. "This sure is easier to handle with someone on my side," LaTonya said.

Points to Consider

Why do you think breathing slowly and deeply is a key factor for a person who has panic disorder?

What do you think is likely to happen if people who have panic disorder pay attention to their symptoms?

Why is it important for a support person to be educated about panic attacks, panic disorder, and treatment?

Why do you think patience is important when trying to help a person with panic disorder?

Glossary

agoraphobia (uh-gor-uh-FOH-bee-uh)—a fear of public places; avoidance of a particular place or situation because of fear of having a panic attack there.

anticipatory anxiety (an-TI-suh-puh-tor-ee ang-ZYE-uh-tee)—extreme fear or dread of having future panic attacks

antidepressant (an-tee-di-PRESS-uhnt)—a drug that prevents or relieves persistent feelings of sadness or despair; often used to relieve the symptoms of panic disorder.

anxiety (ang-ZYE-uh-tee)—an uneasy feeling about something that might happen

avoidance behavior (uh-VOID-uhnss bi-HAYV-yuhr)—avoiding people, places, or situations that a person believes may trigger his or her panic attacks

cognitive behavioral therapy (CBT) (KOG-nuh-tiv bi-HAYV-yuh-rel THER-uh-pee)—panic disorder treatment that helps people discover and correct faulty beliefs and teaches behaviors to reduce anxiety

depression (di-PRESH-uhn)—a mood disorder that includes feelings of intense sadness and hopelessness

heredity (huh-RED-uh-tee)—passing along certain traits from parents to children through genes

panic attack (PAN-ik uh-TAK)—a sudden, overwhelming fear that comes without warning and without any present danger or threat; the most extreme form of anxiety.

panic disorder (PAN-ik diss-OR-dur)—a treatable mental illness whose key symptoms are repeated panic attacks and continuing concern about having another panic attack

phobia (FOH-bee-uh)—an exaggerated and unreasonable continuing fear of a particular object or situation

self-talk (SELF-TAWK)—what we say to ourselves in our own mind

stimulant (STIM-yuh-luhnt)—a substance that produces a temporary increase in certain bodily functions

For More Information

Bodian, Stephen. *Meditation for Dummies.* Foster City, CA: IDG Books Worldwide, 1999.

Bourne, Edmund J. *The Anxiety and Phobia Workbook.* Rev. ed. Oakland, CA: New Harbinger, 2000.

Heller, Sharon. *The Complete Idiot's Guide to Conquering Fear and Anxiety.* New York: Macmillan, 1999.

Monroe, Judy. *Phobias: Everything You Wanted to Know, But Were Afraid to Ask.* Springfield, NJ: Enslow, 1996.

Wilson, R. Reid. *Don't Panic: Taking Control of Anxiety Attacks.* Chapel Hill, NC: Pathway Systems, 1996.

Useful Addresses and Internet Sites

American Academy of Child & Adolescent Psychiatry (AACAP)
3615 Wisconsin Avenue Northwest
Washington, DC 20016-3007
1-800-333-7636
www.aacap.org

American Psychiatric Association (APA)
1400 K Street Northwest
Washington, DC 20005
1-888-357-7924
www.psych.org

Anxiety Disorders Association of America (ADAA)
11900 Parklawn Drive, Suite 100
Rockville, MD 20852-2624
www.adaa.org

Canadian Mental Health Association
2160 Yonge Street, Third Floor
Toronto, ON M4S 2Z3
CANADA
www.cmha.ca

National Anxiety Foundation
3135 Custer Drive
Lexington, KY 40517-4001
www.lexington-on-line.com/naf.panic1.html

National Institute of Mental Health
6001 Executive Boulevard, Room 8184
MSC 9663
Bethesda, MD 20892-9663
www.nimh.nih.gov

National Mental Health Association (NMHA)
1021 Prince Street
Alexandria, VA 22314-2971
1-800-969-6642
www.nmha.org

Anxiety Disorder—The Caregiver
www.pacificcoast.net/~kstrong
Provides information and support to the caregivers of people who have panic attacks

The Anxiety Network International: The Panic Disorder Homepage
www.anxietynetwork.com/pdhome.html
Contains many articles about panic and agoraphobia

The Anxiety Panic Internet Resource
www.algy.com/anxiety/panic.html
Contains online bulletin boards for discussion and support, as well as a newsletter

Freedom From Fear
www.freedomfromfear.com
Provides information on anxiety disorders and depression, includes tips for health and well-being

StudyWeb: Science—Panic Disorder
www.studyweb.com/links/833.html
Has many links to sites that discuss panic disorder

Index

Index continued